PLANT-TASTIC!
OUCH!
PRICKLY PLANTS

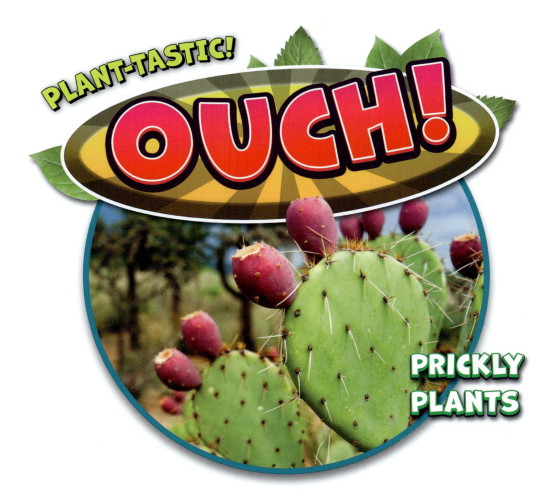

BY REX RUBY

Minneapolis, Minnesota

Credits
Cover and title page, © fotobieshutterb/Adobe Stock and © sara_winter/iStock; 4, © P24_Design/Shutterstock; 4–5, © Charles T. Peden/Shutterstock; 6, © Victor Jiang/Shutterstock; 7, © Danita Delimont/Shutterstock; 8–9, © Tom Fenske/Adobe Stock; 9, © CellarStorm/Adobe Stock; 10, © Carl DeAbreu Photography/Shutterstock; 11, © Brenda Brooks/Shutterstock; 12–13, © Patrik Stedrak/Adobe Stock; 14–15, © Maria Usanina/iStock; 15, © ncox1585/iStock; 16, © Steve Holroyd/Alamy; 16–17, © Linda_K/Shutterstock and © Denis-Huot/Nature Picture Library/Alamy; 18, © msgrafixx/Shutterstock; 19, © Bildagentur Zoonar GmbH/Shutterstock; 20, © USO/iStock; 20–21, © Can/Adobe Stock; 22, © Joe_Potato/iStock, © rusm/iStock, © Lezh/iStock, and © Anastasiia Burlakova/iStock; and 23, © trevorkloz/iStock.

Bearport Publishing Company Product Development Team
President: Jen Jenson; Director of Product Development: Spencer Brinker; Managing Editor: Allison Juda; Associate Editor: Naomi Reich; Senior Designer: Colin O'Dea; Associate Designer: Elena Klinkner; Associate Designer: Kayla Eggert; Product Development Specialist: Anita Stasson

Library of Congress Cataloging-in-Publication Data

Names: Ruby, Rex, author.
Title: Ouch! : prickly plants / by Rex Ruby.
Description: Minneapolis, Minnesota : Bearport Publishing Company, [2024] | Series: Plant-tastic! | Includes bibliographical references and index.
Identifiers: LCCN 2022058248 (print) | LCCN 2022058249 (ebook) | ISBN 9798888220412 (library binding) | ISBN 9798888222348 (paperback) | ISBN 9798888223567 (ebook)
Subjects: LCSH: Plant defenses--Juvenile literature.
Classification: LCC QK921 .R83 2024 (print) | LCC QK921 (ebook) | DDC 581.4/7--dc23/eng/20221209
LC record available at https://lccn.loc.gov/2022058248
LC ebook record available at https://lccn.loc.gov/2022058249

Copyright © 2024 Bearport Publishing Company. All rights reserved. No part of this publication may be reproduced in whole or in part, stored in any retrieval system, or transmitted in any form or by any means, electronic, mechanical, photocopying, recording, or otherwise, without written permission from the publisher.

For more information, write to Bearport Publishing, 5357 Penn Avenue South, Minneapolis, MN 55419.

CONTENTS

A Bite to Eat 4
Prickly Protection 6
Thirsty Plants 8
Spines for Shade 10
Pretty Thorns 12
A Giraffe's Dinner 14
Thorns as Homes 16
Stinging Hairs 18
Don't Touch! 20

Science Lab 22
Glossary 23
Index 24
Read More 24
Learn More Online 24
About the Author 24

A BITE TO EAT

A hungry deer is looking for food in the **desert**. It spots one of the few plants that can survive in this hot, dry place. But will the deer dare to nibble at the juicy cactus? No! The plant has a spiky way to stay safe.

Most cacti grow in rocky or sandy deserts that get very little rain.

PRICKLY PROTECTION

Plants can't move away from danger, such as a hungry animal looking for a treat. So, some plants have a different form of **protection**. They grow sharp **thorns** or **spines** that can poke or scratch anything that comes close.

Thorns grow from branches, and spines come from what would otherwise be leaves.

A thorn

THIRSTY PLANTS

Some of the most well-known prickly plants are cacti. These desert plants have spines to help protect their water-filled stems. For most things living in the desert, water is difficult to find. But cacti can soak up and store gallons of water in their thick, fleshy stems. Spines keep thirsty animals away.

Saguaro (suh-WAH-*roh*) are a very large type of cactus. They can weigh as much as an elephant.

A saguaro

SPINES FOR SHADE

Being prickly helps cacti survive in another important way, too. It keeps them cool! When the sun shines on a cactus, each spine creates a little shadow on the plant's stem. Together, all the spines make lots of shade. This shade keeps the cactus from losing too much water to **evaporation**.

A teddy bear cholla cactus has thousands of spines that make the plant look fuzzy—like a teddy bear.

PRETTY THORNS

Cacti aren't the only plants that prick. Rosebushes have hundreds of tiny thorns. Hard points grow on the stems of these pretty plants and protect their sweet-smelling flowers from hungry animals. Without flowers, roses couldn't make seeds to grow new plants.

Roses can live for a very long time. One of the oldest living rosebushes is over a thousand years old!

A GIRAFFE'S DINNER

Acacia (uh-KAY-shuh) trees have long thorns to protect their tasty leaves. The thorns grow in pairs and stop most hungry animals. However, the trees' thorns are no match for giraffes. The animals use their long tongues to bend around thorns to grab a mouthful of leaves.

Most acacia trees have thorns that are about 4 inches (10 cm) long. That's about as long as a toilet paper roll.

THORNS AS HOMES

Thorns aren't the only way some acacia trees avoid being eaten. Whistling acacia trees get a little help from stinging ants, too. Ants make cozy homes in rounded parts of the thorns and feed on the tree's sweet **sap**. If another animal tries to eat the leaves, the ants sting the creature's tongue and mouth.

These trees get their name from the whistling noise they make when wind blows over the holes on their thorns.

A whistling acacia tree thorn with ants

STINGING HAIRS

Some plants don't need any help stinging. Stinging nettles have tiny, needlelike hairs to protect themselves. Each hair is filled with painful **chemicals**. If an animal touches the leaves or stems, the tiny hairs break off and pump the stinging liquid into the would-be attacker.

The hairs on stinging nettles can be seen if you look closely.

If stung too many times, an animal can die from a stinging nettle plant!

DON'T TOUCH!

Though you don't want to get poked, sometimes a plant's prickly protection can be helpful to people. Thorned plants around a house or garden make a good fence to keep away unwanted visitors. Whatever their use, these plants all give the same warning—don't touch!

Spines and thorns don't stop all animals. Land iguanas eat prickly pear cacti—spines and all!

SCIENCE LAB
PRICKLY SHOW AND TELL

Make a model of a spiny cactus to show how spines help the plant survive.

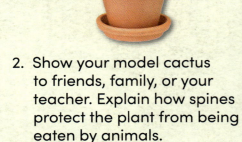

1. Use green modeling clay to make a cactus stem and place it in a pot filled with sand or garden soil. Then, push toothpicks into the clay for spines.

2. Show your model cactus to friends, family, or your teacher. Explain how spines protect the plant from being eaten by animals.

3. Put the cactus in a sunny place to see if the spines make shadows. Explain how these shadows help keep a cactus cool.

GLOSSARY

chemicals natural substances that can sometimes be harmful to living things

desert a place that gets very little rain and where very few plants and animals can survive

evaporation the process by which a liquid, such as water, changes into a gas

protection something that keeps someone or something safe

sap a liquid that flows through a plant and carries water and food for the plant

spines hard, sharp, needlelike growths on some plants

thorns sharp points on the branches or stems of some plants

INDEX

ants 16–17
cacti 4, 8–10, 12, 20, 22
deserts 4, 8
giraffes 14
hairs 18
rosebushes 12
shade 10
spines 6–8, 10, 20, 22
stems 8, 10, 12, 18, 22
thorns 6, 12–17, 20
trees 14–17
water 8, 10

READ MORE

Griffin, Mary. *Prickly Desert Cacti (Fantastic Plants)*. New York: PowerKids Press, 2023.

Levy, Janey. *African Acacia Trees Protect Themselves! (World's Weirdest Plants)*. New York: Gareth Stevens Publishing, 2020.

Machajewski, Sarah. *How Plants Protect Themselves (The Top Secret Life of Plants)*. New York: Gareth Stevens Publishing, 2020.

LEARN MORE ONLINE

1. Go to **www.factsurfer.com** or scan the QR code below.
2. Enter "**Ouch**" into the search box.
3. Click on the cover of this book to see a list of websites.

ABOUT THE AUTHOR

Rex Ruby lives in Minnesota with his family. Although he knows better, he doesn't always stay away from prickly plants.